The 60-Minute Guide to

Building the Infrastructure for Successful Nonprofit Fundraising

10 Essential Building Blocks for
Nonprofit Fundraising

TRACY VANDERNECK, MSM, CFRE

BUILDING THE INFRASTRUCTURE FOR SUCCESSFUL NONPROFIT FUNDRAISING

Copyright © 2024 Phil-Com, LLC
All rights reserved.
ISBN: 979-8-218-43450-2

A MESSAGE TO READERS

This book is a tool that can be used by nonprofit organizations and nongovernmental organizations to help establish the robust infrastructure that is needed for successful fundraising efforts. *It is not a how-to on fundraising itself;* you will not find descriptions of how to write a fundraising appeal or ask for funds. What you will find is help on how to take the steps necessary to create a fundraising program that is built to last and to help your organization achieve its goals. You can ask supporters for funds anytime, but unless you have the right strategic support tools in place, there is much less chance of satisfied investors and repeat donations.

Whether your nonprofit is well established and needs to make changes to improve your strategic fundraising efforts, or you are newly formed and building a development (fundraising) department from the ground up, **Building the Infrastructure for Successful Nonprofit Fundraising** is the resource for you.

The concepts in this book have been subjected to an open peer review process by other fundraising practitioners to help ensure that you as the reader are receiving the best tools to help your organization have a successful fundraising journey. No content was generated using artificial intelligence (AI).

You have chosen to be a part of an incredibly rewarding profession. **The 10 Essential Building Blocks for Nonprofit Fundraising** are here to help you succeed in funding the missions you care about.

Tracy Vanderneck

Tracy Vanderneck, MSM, CFRE
President, Phil-Com

The information in this book should not be considered legal or financial advice.

Contents

GETTING STARTED 5
    FUNDRAISING INFRASTRUCTURE MODEL, Figure 1. 7

CHAPTER 1 9
    Building Block - Case for Support 9
    CASE FOR SUPPORT SAMPLE OUTLINE, Figure 2. 11
    MEASUREMENTS OF MISSION SUCCESS, Figure 3. 12

CHAPTER 2 13
    Building Block - Culture of Philanthropy 13

CHAPTER 3 15
    Building Block - Staffing 15

CHAPTER 4 17
    Building Block - Goals & Budgeting 17
    FUNDING VS FUNDRAISING, Figure 4. 17
    ORGANIZATIONAL BUDGET ILLUSTRATION, Figure 5. 19
    YEAR-TO-YEAR COMPARISON FOR PROJECTIONS ILLUSTRATION, Figure 6. 20

CHAPTER 5 23
    Building Block - Technology 23

CHAPTER 6 27
    Building Block - Development Plans & Methods 27
    ORDER OF STRATEGIC WORKFLOW, Figure 7. 27
    DEVELOPMENT PLAN SAMPLE, Figure 8. 28
    DEVELOPMENT PLAN CREATION PROCESS, Figure 9. 29

CHAPTER 7 31
    Building Block - Performance Indicators 31
    FUNDRAISING METRICS, Figure 10. 32
    COMPARISON METRICS, Figure 11. 32
    EVENT METRICS, Figure 12. 33
    APPEAL* METRICS, Figure 13. 33
    RETURN ON INVESTMENT, Figure 14. 34

COST PER DOLLAR RAISED, Figure 15. 34
CHAPTER 8 35
   Building Block - Development Committee 35
CHAPTER 9 37
   Building Block - Policies, Procedures, & Ethics 37
CHAPTER 10 43
   Building Block - Fundraising Evolution 43
   HUMAN FOCUSED FUNDRAISING TRIAD, Figure 16. 47
SUMMARY 49
GLOSSARY 51
REFERENCES 55

GETTING STARTED

Nonprofit organizations, also known as not-for-profit organizations (NPO) and nongovernmental organizations (NGO), serve a wide range of functions. They all hold some level of tax-exempt status and, as a group, comprise the Independent Sector. Organizations' purposes vary so widely, however, that the sector is often segmented into categories based on the type of service provided. A few examples of such segmentation are organizations that:

- provide life-saving services to animals (Animal Welfare)
- bring arts and cultural experiences to communities (Arts & Culture)
- represent groups of people, such as membership societies, associations, and unions (Associations & Service Clubs)
- provide educational offerings (Education)
- preserve the environment and natural resources (Environmental)
- provide grant-making services (Foundations)
- offer faith-based teaching or services (Religion)
- address societal inequities (Social Justice)
- serve as a safety net for humans in need (Social/Human Services)

One thing all nonprofit organizations have in common is that they must secure funding in order to fulfill their missions and deliver services. The ways in which nonprofits fund their missions are always evolving. As of 2024, some of the most popular and/or effective ways are:

- philanthropic giving from individuals in small, medium, and large denominations, including gifts made by bequests in wills and trusts
- partnerships with and sponsorships from corporations, including social enterprises and cause marketing
- hosting special events
- grants from foundations and corporations
- contracts or funding from government agencies
- income from the sale of goods or services

Whatever methods nonprofit organizations use to pursue funding to support their mission delivery, they must be professional, strategic, ethical, and transparent to be effective. **The following pages describe how you can build the framework for a**

successful, thriving fundraising program at a nonprofit organization. *This book focuses on the basis for philanthropic fundraising, so funding from government agencies and any types of earned income through the sale of products or services will not be addressed.*

The necessary framework is described in the **10 Essential Building Blocks for Nonprofit Fundraising**. Let's begin with an overview of the components as shown in Figure 1. on the following page. Then each subsequent chapter will take a closer look at the individual components. Spending the next 60 minutes learning what you need to do to be successful in fundraising for your nonprofit through philanthropic means will be time invested wisely!

FUNDRAISING INFRASTRUCTURE MODEL, Figure 1.

10 ESSENTIAL BUILDING BLOCKS FOR NONPROFIT FUNDRAISING

case for support

The organization must be able to articulate its reason for being - the issues it exists to address, how it meets those needs, and what resources are necessary to accomplish the work.

culture of philanthropy

Organizational commitment, beginning with the board of directors and ED/CEO, to positively integrate fundraising into every aspect of the organization.

staffing

It is ideal to have at least one employee (or volunteer for small nonprofits) whose role is largely dedicated to fundraising, who works closely with the board of directors to raise funds in a professional and strategic manner.

goals & budgeting

The best indicator of current ability to raise philanthropic dollars is past performance. Even for a start-up organization, fundraising goals should be based on realistic organizational budgets and must be grounded in reality.

technology

Fundraising is a professional process with industry standards and best practices. The appropriate technology is a must for any successful development department.

development methods & plans

There are many ways to raise funds. Use a combination of methods and follow a sound strategy. A development plan should match the direction defined in the organization's strategic plan and adhere to an ethical fundraising methodology.

performance indicators

Fundraising methods must be continually analyzed for efficiency and effectiveness, including funds raised, cost to raise a dollar, number of new donors, number of returning donors, and increased gift amounts.

development committee

A development committee works with staff to raise philanthropic dollars, evaluate strategy, and champion development efforts with the board of directors. A development committee is not the same thing as a special event committee and does not replace each board member's individual role in fundraising.

policies, procedures, and ethics

Organizations must have appropriate policies & procedures in place, know and adhere to regulations, and have strong dedication to professional ethics and equity in fundraising.

fundraising evolution

Organizations must continually monitor the philanthropic sector to keep current with evolving philosophies and methods of engaging supporters.

©2024 Phil-Com, LLC

CHAPTER 1
Building Block - Case for Support

A Case for Support is one of the most important tools for fundraising that an organization can have. It is the articulation of the reason that the nonprofit organization exists and why it deserves philanthropic support. In its most basic form, a Case for Support is a printed or electronic document that is usually several pages long. It may simply be a well-formatted PDF, or it can be professionally graphically designed.

Regardless of the type of design you choose, a Case for Support is used as an information-sharing tool with potential financial supporters who have the capacity and inclination to invest in the nonprofit at significant levels.

Once the full-length printed/electronic format is complete, the information in the Case for Support can be used as the basis to create additional tools such as content for grant applications, educational infographics, informational videos, commentary for virtual tours, and marketing brochures.

> **CASE FOR SUPPORT**
>
> A document that articulates the reason your nonprofit organization exists and why it is worthy of philanthropic support.

A solid Case for Support answers the questions of:

- Why does the organization need to exist? What situation or problem exists in the community that will be addressed, made better, or fixed because of the work of this organization?
- Why is the organization considered valid to deliver this mission? Who does the organization have that makes it the right one to deliver on the specific services? For example, does the staff hold excellent credentials? Does your combined knowledge and lived experience give you the know-how to deliver on the mission at the highest level?
- How will you address the need in the community? Is it a program, a research study, a specific-use building, or something else?
    - How will you make it happen?
    - How will you fund implementation and ongoing operations?

- What results or improvements will be achieved by those served by this organization's mission delivery, programs, services, or projects? What is the expected impact?
- What resources do you need to make this solution a reality? What does the budget look like for the organization to be well-run or for the project to be accomplished in the best way possible – not the cheapest way, the best way?
- Whether or not there is an expected timeframe for the project, and if so, what is that timeframe?

The process of answering the questions above to create the Case for Support has the added benefits of:
- Helping the board and staff come to a consensus about the specific needs that the organization addresses
- Creating a standardized way that the board and staff communicate regarding the mission both within the organization and externally to constituents and the community
- Showing what funds are needed to deliver on the mission

It can be easy for the founders of new nonprofits to carry the vision for the organization in their mind, but harder for them to document it all in a way that helps other people understand the need, the proposed solution, and the resources needed to make the vision a reality. A Case for Support is the tool that helps make the vision a reality.

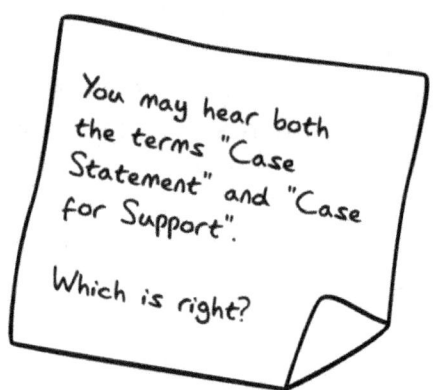

You may hear both the terms "Case Statement" and "Case for Support". Which is right?

CASE STATEMENT VS CASE FOR SUPPORT

A CASE STATEMENT is a short summary, generally a sentence or two, that describes the reason the organization exists.

A CASE FOR SUPPORT is a full document that is longer and contains more specific information on the need or situation that exists in the community. It articulates the reason the nonprofit exists and includes details that show why financial support of the mission or project is worthwhile.

BUILDING THE INFRASTRUCTURE FOR SUCCESSFUL NONPROFIT FUNDRAISING

Though all Cases for Support may look different, they tend to follow the same general outline and include similar components, such as shown in Figure 2. below.

CASE FOR SUPPORT SAMPLE OUTLINE, Figure 2.

Outline

SAMPLE CASE FOR SUPPORT

I. Mission of the organization

II. Vision of the organization or the specific project for which you are writing the case

III. The situation or problem to be addressed
   a. What is the general background? How are things now?
      Example: Over 2,000 people are homeless/unhoused in xxx county.
   b. What is the issue that your organizational mission or the specific project addresses?
      Example: The physical health of the homeless individuals.
         i. Depending on the complexity of the issue, it may be reasonable to separate this description under subheadings.
         Example: Medical, dental, emotional, mental health, basic human rights.

IV. The financial impact the problem has on the community
   a. How is the problem costing the community money, or keeping it from making money?
      Example: If the homeless/unhoused people in the county have medical issues, they will likely be served through indigent care programs at local hospitals, which may be funded through taxes.

V. Your organization's solution
   a. What will you do, or are you doing, to help assuage the problem?

VI. Financial impact solution
      Example: If the medical needs of the homeless/unhoused population are addressed through your organization's program, the people who are homeless are less likely to use indigent care programs at local hospitals, thus requiring less taxpayer money to fund those programs.

VII. What does the organization need in order to make the solution a reality?
      Example: $xxx would provide xxx number of people with help or have xxx type of impact.

VIII. A budget breakdown of the proposed program

IX. An appeal for funds
   a. In some cases, when this tool is being used for major donors at high level gifts in the campaign, you can also include a "gift pyramid" here. A gift pyramid is a breakdown of how many gifts you will need at each monetary level to successfully fund the project.
   b. Include wording that requests funds.

©2024 Phil-Com, LLC   www.phil-com.com

When drafting or sharing the message of your Case for Support, it is important to be able to explain/show the difference your solution will make, the impact it will have. The graphic below breaks down the ways you can describe that difference.

MEASUREMENTS OF MISSION SUCCESS, Figure 3.

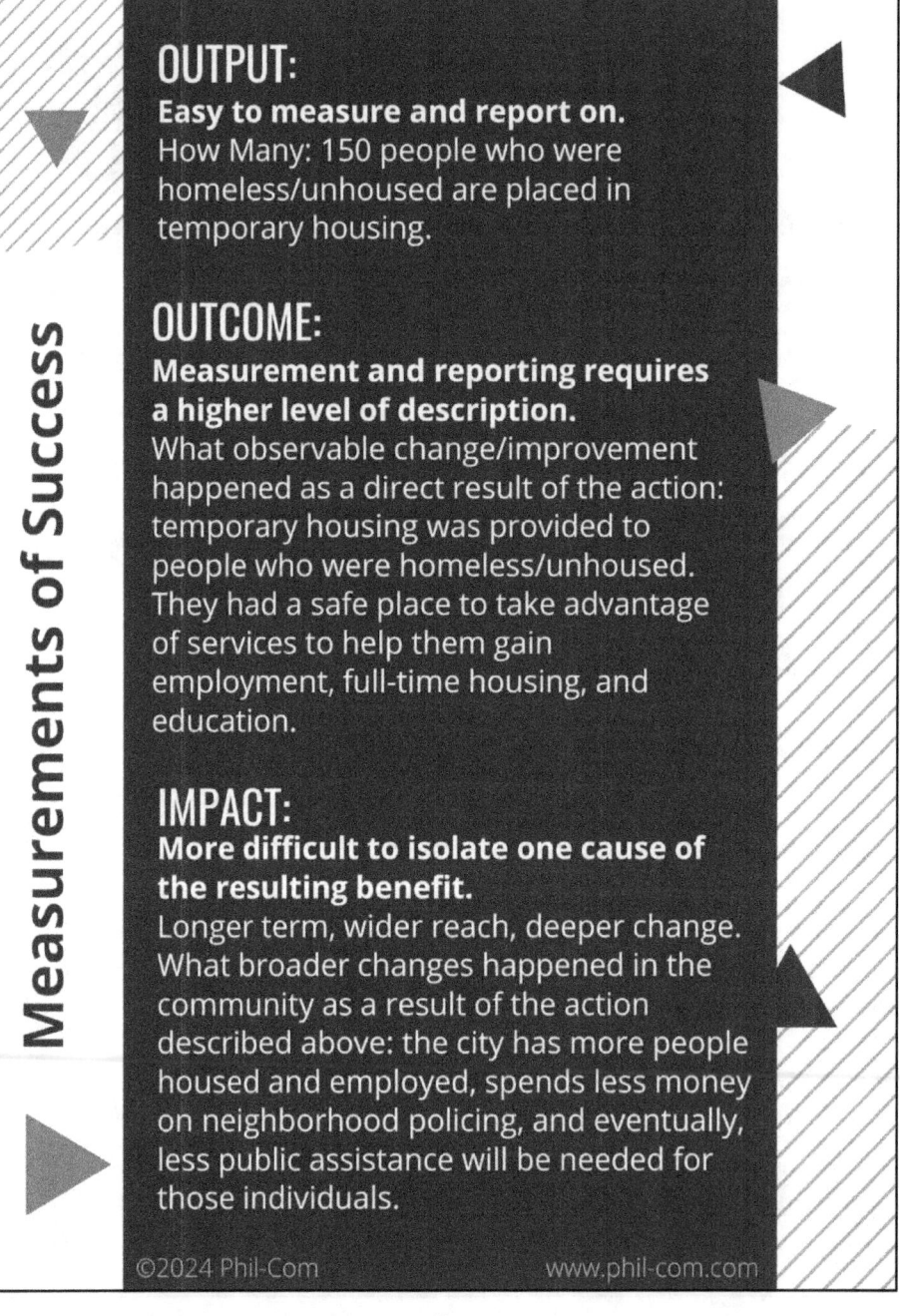

CHAPTER 2
Building Block - Culture of Philanthropy

Philanthropic culture is a subset of organizational culture. A culture of philanthropy[i] refers to the organization's **overall attitude towards fund development (fundraising)**. It is an organizational commitment, beginning with the board of directors and the Chief Executive Officer/Executive Director (CEO/ED), to positively integrate fundraising into every aspect of the organization. (If your organization operates in a horizontal cooperative model, a culture of philanthropy is still very important; it just means that everyone in the co-op model must equally believe in the benefit of integrated philanthropy).

Weaving a positive fundraising culture into the fabric of the organization *does not* mean that fundraising becomes more important than everything else. It *does* mean that board members and staff make a continual effort to connect fundraising to mission delivery. One of the biggest components of this is for everyone involved to be willing to share the story of the organization's mission with their own networks of friends, family, colleagues, and community members.

Young Organizations' Cultures of Philanthropy

New and small nonprofits, especially ones run predominantly by volunteers, can find fundraising overwhelming and even a bit embarrassing at first. They may feel awkward asking their friends, family, colleagues, and the community to support the work of the nonprofit. This discomfort may cause them to act in a way that is contrary to a positive culture of philanthropy – they may inadvertently create a culture of avoidance.

There is no need to feel anxious about fundraising. Do you believe strongly in the mission of your organization? Are you passionate about it? Do you believe that once other people learn about the impact that the work of the organization has, they are likely to believe it is important too? If your answers are yes, you're starting in the right place! It would, however, be ill-advised to believe that *everyone* you tell about your mission will automatically want to support it. Keep in mind that many people already have missions they care about and to which they donate, so they may or may not be able to donate to your organization too,

even if they feel you have a compelling mission. But they won't have the chance to give unless you ask them!

Many people want to support the work of certain missions but aren't sure how to go about it. If you, as a representative of the organization, share highlights from the Case for Support, show examples of positive impact, share that you personally have already given financial support, and ask people to give, you're creating a way for them to help. You're acting as a conduit between people who want to help and the missions that need financial support.

CHAPTER 3
Building Block - Staffing

Organizations often take the time, both at inception and throughout the life of the agency, to plan for staffing needs in *programs and mission delivery* based on relevant expert guidance, but they don't always apply the same formulas to creating a map for successful *fund development*.

It is imperative for any organization that wants to create a successful fundraising program to plan and forecast from where your funding will come, as well as what staff will be needed to conduct the associated work. It should not be an afterthought, but an important part of your business plan and strategic plan.

Fundraising is a profession. The existence of the following characteristics is what, under common understanding, qualifies fundraising to be defined as a profession. There is:
- expert knowledge with a theoretical base acquired by a lengthy period of training
- a demonstrated devotion to marrying technical knowledge with human relationships
- an active professional association
- a code of ethics
- a high level of control over credentialing and application of the work

Fundraising meets these requirements and there are scores of dedicated professionals that do this important work. However, development professionals cannot do the work alone. They need leaders who will educate themselves about industry standards and best practices, and who will actively build a culture of philanthropy where a dedication to professional, equitable, and ethical fundraising permeates every level of the organization. It is imperative that organizations commit to the time, effort, planning, resources, and execution necessary for long-term success in fundraising.

Hire the Right People for the Right Jobs

An important part of building a fund development program is to make sure you have the right people doing the right jobs and that you are compensating them at an appropriate level for the industry and their experience. Additionally, as of 2024, salary transparency is becoming the norm for fundraising positions in an effort to increase pay equity among all practitioners. Here are a few examples of the type of staff positions you may employ to forward your fundraising goals:

- At a new, young, or volunteer-led organization, you will likely have one or two volunteers that take responsibility for spearheading fundraising. This is a terrific start and these volunteers should engage in training and continuing education to learn about the art and science of fundraising. By doing so, they can help ensure the *organization creates positive fund development habits from the very beginning*.
- As organizations grow, they are likely to hire dedicated development staff. They may start out with a part-time person with the goal of having at least one full-time fundraiser. Eventually, development departments grow to the point where they have staff members dedicated to each specific type of philanthropic support solicitation.
- Regardless of the size of the organization, it is important to also have someone dedicated to being the point person for processing donations and maintaining a database of current and future donors (we will cover the database in Chapter 5). This person should participate in ongoing training that will teach them donor data management industry standards, as well as how to track donor intent and ensure there is proper attention paid to donor privacy.

Desirable Attitude and Skills

As the industry evolves, fundraising will continue to become even more nuanced. The types of relationships nonprofits have with donors, clients, and the communities in which they operate, and the way those relationships are stewarded, will metamorphize over time to become more equitable and encompassing (we'll cover more about partnership-based fundraising in Chapter 10).

When budgeting, it is a good idea to include not only fair/good compensation, but also continuing education dollars for your staff to help them remain as current as possible. When hiring, try to find appropriately representative professionals that are willing and able to adapt as the world and the way people interact with nonprofits changes.

Just like there is no single right way of raising money from all types of funders (for example, an organization's entire development program should not rely upon applying for the same grants from the same funders every single year), there is also not just one professional view of how fundraising should be accomplished. Strategic adaptability is a fantastic trait in a fundraising professional.

CHAPTER 4
Building Block - Goals & Budgeting

This book is mainly focused on creating the infrastructure for *fundraising* (the right side of Figure 4. below). However, when budgeting for the year or projecting budgets for future years of the organization, you will need to include all types of *funding* (the left side of Figure 4.). We briefly covered it in the "Getting Started" section of this book, but let's take a minute to revisit the topic and make the distinction clear by defining the difference between funding and fundraising:

FUNDING VS FUNDRAISING, Figure 4.

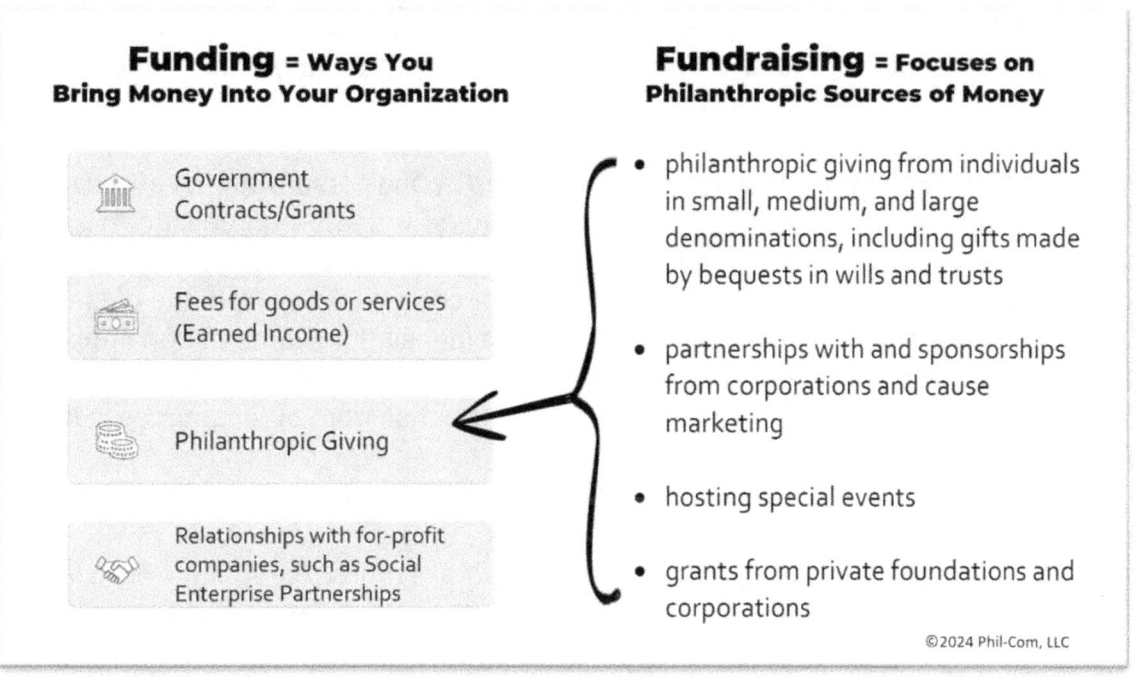

New Organizations

Brand-new nonprofit organizations should have a business plan that includes expense projections for at least the first three years of operations. You must be able to answer the questions:

- What mission *exactly* are you planning to deliver with what types of services or programs?
- What physical and human resources do you need to make it happen?
- What will those resources cost?
    - Create an organizational budget that projects all expenses, including resource materials, facilities rental if needed, insurance, technology, salaries if there will be any in the first few years, and any other relevant items.
- What is your plan to scale the building of the business in the first three or more years?

Once you have the expenses set, you can then begin considering the ways you will work to secure funding and add income projections to the budget. You may have to adjust your expectations along the way. Your budget should also include an allocation for the costs of fundraising.

Many start-up nonprofits, especially those founded by one person, cannot afford to pay an executive director for the *first two to three years*; it can be unrealistic to expect otherwise. If your model does require any paid staff right away, then you must plan to seek funding that will cover staff and/or contractor compensation from the outset and then have a plan for future coverage of that staff expense (for example, don't apply for a grant to pay a staff position for year one of the organization's operations without having a plan for how you're going to sustain that expense from other sources in future years).

More Established Organizations
If your organization has been operating for a few years or more, use your previous years' numbers as a starting place for projecting what you can raise in the coming year. (Shown in Figures 5. and 6.)

Drafting the Budget

Organizational budgets have two sections – revenue and expenses. Creating a budget for the entire agency is an important part of the process, because *you must know what you need in order to effectively ask for philanthropic monetary support to make it happen.*

ORGANIZATIONAL BUDGET ILLUSTRATION, Figure 5.

	Previous Year Budgeted	Previous Year Actual	Current Year Budgeted	Current Year Actual as of XXX Date
Revenue				
Earned Income/Sales	$50,000	$51,400	$57,500	$36,200
Gov't Contracts	$150,000	$150,000	$134,000	$120,000
Contributions	$100,000	$96,500	$115,000	$75,000
Subtotal Revenue	$300,000	$297,900	$306,500	$231,200
Expenses				
Insurance	$15,000	$17,500	$17,500	$13,125
Payroll	$85,000	$89,000	$89,000	$66,750
Program Materials	$200,000	$201,250	$200,000	$150,000
Subtotal Expenses	$300,000	$307,750	$306,500	$229,875
Balance	$0	($9,850)	$0	$1,325

Figure 5. is a highly simplified illustration. There are many places online where you can access free budget templates for nonprofit organizations that will help you define your own income and expenses by line item. One source I find useful are the templates offered by The New Hampshire Center for Nonprofits[ii] (www.nhnonprofits.org).

Forming Projections

It is a good idea to project modest, achievable increases in contributions, such as 15% to 25% over the previous year or the average of previous years. Do not project a 100% increase in your fundraising goal unless there is an identifiable catalyst that could realistically make that happen. If there were certain years that had large increases or decreases in fundraising due to unusual circumstances (e.g., pandemic-related fundraising, or a natural disaster), take those anomalies into account when forecasting. If you had one year where fundraising was much higher because of a one-time, *nonrenewable* grant, it is not reasonable to forecast using that higher number as your baseline for what is achievable.

Let's take a look at a sample three-year fundraising comparison that shows how you can use the previous three years' information to project philanthropic income for budget purposes, in Figure 6.

YEAR-TO-YEAR COMPARISON FOR PROJECTIONS ILLUSTRATION, Figure 6.

	2021 ACTUAL	2022 ACTUAL	2023 ACTUAL	3-YEAR AVERAGE	2024 PROJECTED (+15%) ★
EMAIL APPEALS	$21,000	$25,000	$22,400	$22,800	$26,220
DIRECT MAIL	$15,600	$17,000	$17,400	$16,667	$19,167
GRANTS	$22,500	$25,000	$22,500	$23,333	$26,833
SOCIAL MEDIA CAMPAIGNS	$12,000	$14,000	$16,000	$14,000	$16,100
MAJOR GIFT ASKS	$50,000	$50,000	$60,000	$53,333	$61,333
SPECIAL EVENTS	$25,000	$29,000	$28,000	$27,333	$32,333
TOTALS	$146,100	$160,000	$166,300	$157,466	$181,086

★ THIS IS A SIMPLIFIED ILLUSTRATION. FOR REAL-LIFE PROJECTIONS, IT IS NOT LIKELY THAT YOU WOULD PROJECT THE EXACT SAME % INCREASE IN ALL CATEGORIES.
→ FOR EXAMPLE, BECAUSE SOCIAL MEDIA CAMPAIGN INCOME HAS BEEN RISING STEADILY EACH YEAR, IT WOULD BE REASONABLE TO PROJECT 15% INCREASE OVER THE HIGHEST YEAR INSTEAD OF OVER THE AVERAGE OF THE LAST THREE YEARS, BUT ONLY IF YOU PLAN TO CONTINUE A STRATEGIC FOCUS ON SOCIAL MEDIA CAMPAIGNS.
→ MAJOR GIFT PROJECTIONS COULD BE SIGNIFICANTLY INFLUENCED BY INFORMATION FROM THE SPECIFIC RESEARCH PROFILES OF YOUR CURRENT/PROSPECTIVE LARGE-GIFT DONORS.

Be realistic. It is okay to have stretch goals but try to avoid *fantastical* goals. You can also include cautious projections for new methods of fundraising you are planning to pilot in the coming year. For example, if you have forged a relationship with a business that plans to run a cause marketing campaign to benefit your organization in the coming year (and they've signed a third-party fundraising agreement so you know it will truly happen), add a line item for it in your fundraising projections.

When adding new fundraising categories to the budget, it is better to under-budget and over-deliver than to plan a goal that is unrealistically high and then have to scramble together money from other sources if that funding does not materialize, or worse, to have to cut planned programming.

It often takes a full year or more from the time concerted fundraising efforts begin for an organization to recognize a sustainable increase in philanthropic dollars. Fundraising is a long game that takes consistent action, solid relationship building, and detailed tracking to be successful. Once the investment in building a development program has been made, it requires loyalty to that course of action for a period of time long enough to see the positive results.

> There is a difference between forecasting in a strategic and ambitious way and forecasting unrealistically. It is okay to have a goal and a "stretch" goal, but if your overall fundraising goal is artificially inflated and not grounded in reality, you are setting your organization up for failure. This type of goal setting can end up being demotivating to fundraising staff and volunteers who can never hit the target number.

CHAPTER 5
Building Block - Technology

All nonprofit organizations need standard business technology like computers/laptops/tablets, networking infrastructure, desktop software, cloud-based storage, remote work capabilities, cybersecurity tools, program delivery-related software, accounting software, and other relevant apps and tools. When budgeting, these items should be considered a necessity, not a luxury.

Technology Built for Fundraising is a Must
In addition to the enterprise-wide tech mentioned above, successful strategic fundraising requires its own dedicated technology.

Fundraising entails a great deal of data management. It involves securely storing correct contact information, accepting online and in-person donations, documenting gifts, acknowledging and providing tax receipts for donations, segmenting lists of supporters and prospective supporters, targeting messaging, communicating mission stories and impact, and integration of these various functions in as seamless a way as possible.

The main tool organizations need for successful fundraising is a system that organizes and integrates data management, gift processing, and communication needs. These systems are often described interchangeably as:

- Constituent Relationship Management (CRM)
- Customer Relationship Management (CRM)
- Donor Relationship Management (DRM)

It can be daunting to find the right system for your organization, so here are a few tips. The best thing you can do is research the companies that describe their services as being a CRM, DRM, or more generically as a "fundraising system". Then narrow down the list by identifying which systems offer specific features and benefits (keep in mind that technology changes fast, so this list will also be ever-evolving). You may have to prioritize which features you want the most, depending on your budget. Your basic needs will likely include:
- **Database** that houses all the contact information, gift documentation, and history of actions taken with the person/company on that record

- **Integrated email blast** capabilities that allow you to draft fundraising appeals that include photos and videos and email out directly from the system
- **Artificial Intelligence (AI) integration that** helps integrate and automate various functions
- **Capability to create and merge direct mail appeals**, including photos and information specific to each contact (such as prior year's gift amount)
- **Text-to-Give functions**
- **Gift tracking** that includes the ability to note whether gifts have been given for a specific purpose
- **Integrated donation pages** that can be linked to from your website, social media, newsletters, and other communications
- **The ability to track interactions and schedule tasks and upcoming actions**

Some systems also offer the options to:
- **Track grants** throughout the application and administration process
- **Collect information through integrated forms**
- **Manage volunteers**
- **Manage special events** including ticketing, sponsorships, and auctions
- **Have AI draft appeal language for you**
- **Sync directly with your accounting software** (the majority of systems at this point offer a way to export your giving data that can then be uploaded to or compared with accounting software).

First, identify and list your most desired features/needs, then create a secondary list of items it would "be nice to have". Make a list of the systems that appear to meet those needs as well as your price range. Then schedule product demos with the top three or four vendors on your list.

Keep in mind that though you may be starting small, it is a good idea to select a system that is scalable as your organization and fundraising grow.

The programs/software available on the market have varying levels of complexity. Some have simple user interfaces, and some are built to be used by data experts. The most important thing to do is to select a system that your team will use! If you are a younger or all-volunteer organization, it is probably a good idea to select a system at least partially by ease of use over complexity of function.

Additional Technology
In addition to the integrated ways to use technology for fundraising listed above, there are a number of other ways that are more transactional and less focused on building relationships with supporters. Here are a few examples:
- Roundup donations/Microdonations refers to applications that allow donors to round their retail purchases up to the nearest dollar to benefit a charity
- Social media giving mechanisms, such as donating through Facebook, Instagram, or TikTok
- Giving through links provided in video streaming on channels like YouTube, video gaming by popular players on channels such as Twitch, and social media promotion by influencers across all platforms
- An electronic donation "jar" is basically an electronic version of a charity donation box/bucket that allows people to give using debit or credit cards instead of pennies and quarters

Nonprofits have less control over giving via these mechanisms, but they can still be very valuable ways of engaging technology for fundraising.

CHAPTER 6
Building Block - Development Plans & Methods

What a Development Plan Is
A Development Plan is an internal planning document, created every fiscal year, that is unique to your organization and helps you plan your strategic fundraising efforts. It is a relatively high-level document that describes major actions but does not include task level details. It is like a blueprint that helps you see the big picture of your fundraising goal and the steps you plan to take to get there.

Fundraising actions should always support the desired direction of mission delivery. The Development Plan is a tool for the development team and board of directors, and the items included in it should be in sync with the organization's overall strategic plan.

ORDER OF STRATEGIC WORKFLOW, Figure 7.

What a Development Plan Looks Like
Different people process information in a variety of ways. Some prefer spreadsheet-based information, some prefer more detailed and descriptive documents. Whatever format you choose to use is fine, because *the most important thing is that it is written in a way that your team will actually use it* as a working tool that they are comfortable with.

BUILDING THE INFRASTRUCTURE FOR SUCCESSFUL NONPROFIT FUNDRAISING

 Scan this code to access a free Development Plan Template.

DEVELOPMENT PLAN SAMPLE, Figure 8.

DEVELOPMENT PLAN
FISCAL YEAR DATES _____

TOTAL FUNDRAISING GOAL: $ 500,000

Fundraising categories below should add up to total $ 500,000

FUNDRAISING FROM INDIVIDUALS $ 250,000
   EMAIL APPEALS $ 100,000
   DIRECT MAIL APPEALS $ 100,000
   IN-PERSON ASKS $ 50,000

FUNDRAISING FROM CORPORATIONS $ 100,000
   ANNUAL PARTNERSHIPS $ 100,000

FUNDRAISING FROM FOUNDATIONS $ 100,000
   GRANT 1 $ 50,000
   GRANT 2 $ 50,000

FUNDRAISING FROM SPECIAL EVENTS $ 50,000
   EVENT 1 $ 25,000
   EVENT 2 $ 25,000

Regardless of the design format you choose, it is important that specific details are included.

1. Start with the fiscal year's overall fundraising goal
2. List the fundraising activities the organization will engage in to reach that goal
3. Assign a portion of the overall fundraising goal to each action/type of fundraising
4. Assign who is responsible for each action*
5. Show timeframes for the actions*

*Numbers four and five are not depicted in the graphic to the left.

There are scores of fundraising actions nonprofit organizations can perform to raise funds to support their missions. There are so many ways that it doesn't make sense for an organization, especially a small organization, to try to employ *every* type of fundraising. It is necessary for nonprofits to make **strategic choices** about what types of fundraising they will engage in and when.

Benefits of Creating a Development Plan
An important function of the Development Plan is to help allocate human and financial resources. The plan defines all the fundraising-related actions you expect to take throughout the year and when, thus giving you a starting place from which you can allocate your staff and volunteers to achieve the described work.

It also aids in allocating fundraising budget. For example, if you intend to send three direct mail pieces during the fiscal year, you can create a budget that includes design, printing, and postage for each mailing. If you plan to host two fundraising events, you can add together all of the projected costs of the events (including a percentage of staff salaries based on the time spent on the planning and management of the event), so that you can accurately project *net* revenue from the event.

Using the allocation process described above can help you get a clear picture of where your fundraising budget and staff time will be spent. Then if new fundraising ideas are suggested throughout the year, you can measure them against the current plan to determine if you have enough resources available to add the new idea, or if you would need to stop doing one of the planned actions to engage in a new one.

Who Should Draft the Development Plan?
If your organization has dedicated paid fundraising staff, they should make the first draft of the Development Plan, because they are best positioned to have all of the donor-related information and to understand what resources are available to be allocated. If your organization does not have dedicated fundraising staff, then the CEO/ED is next in line to make the first draft.

It is an important step to have the plan reviewed and approved by the board of directors. As the board of directors is the fundraising staff's best partner in raising funds to support the mission and many fundraising actions require trustee participation, it is a good idea to obtain their buy-in on the planned strategy.

DEVELOPMENT PLAN CREATION PROCESS, Figure 9.

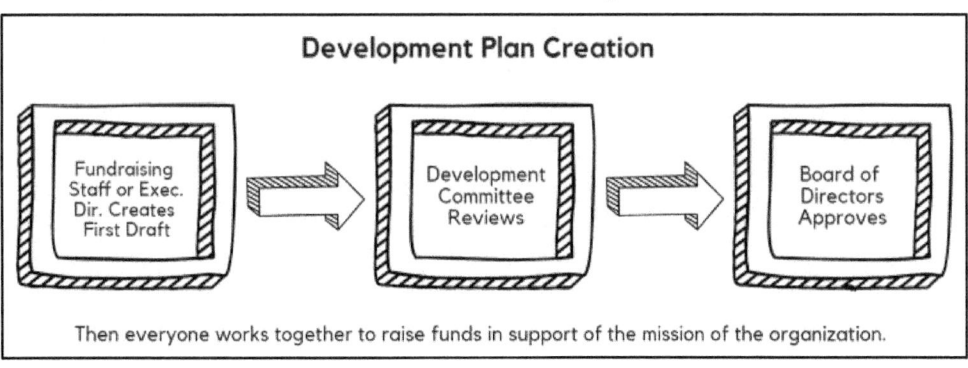

Choose Wisely
It is also important to evaluate each fundraising activity for effectiveness and efficiency to determine which ways of raising funds are working best for your organization. Though the Development Plan does not in and of itself calculate metrics, it is a good place to see all the actions laid out in a succinct way that makes it easy to evaluate each item. Two such evaluations are Return on Investment (ROI) and Cost Per Dollar Raised (CPDR). There is more detail on ROI and CPDR in Chapter 7.

CHAPTER 7
Building Block - Performance Indicators

Earlier chapters described the need to be strategic in planning and executing your organization's fundraising activities. Now let's take a look at the types of things you can measure to determine if what you are doing is working.

The amount of money raised/secured is of course an important measurement, but it isn't the only one. Some larger, more established organizations require a certain number of "contacts" per development professional per week. The contacts may be phone calls, in-person meetings, email – some type of interpersonal interaction. Fundraising relations are, however, about the quality of the interaction and its relevance to the desired outcome.

Grant Metrics
For grant writers, metrics to track may be number of grantors researched, number of Letters of Interest or applications sent, or number of grants secured. However, because most foundations have very specific criteria for what type of organizations and projects they will and will not fund, sheer numbers of applications alone isn't a great performance indicator. It could incent a grant writer to apply to foundations that aren't a perfect fit just to hit the required number of applications. The best indicators related to grants are:
1. Are grants being secured for budget-relieving funds? Meaning, would the organization still need to pay for the item whether or not grant funds are received? Examples of budget-relieving items are staff salaries, a vehicle replacement that is necessary to continue core program operations, or unrestricted dollars to be used where the organization needs them most.
2. Is the organization achieving reasonable increases in grant funding secured? For example, if the organization secured three grants for a total of $15,000 for each of the last three years, a good performance goal would be to secure four or five grants that total $20,000 (a 33.3% increase). Of course, organizations would like their funding from grants to increase at much larger rates. But realism in forecasting is key.

General Fundraising Metrics
It is a good idea for the person(s) responsible for fundraising to evaluate their performance metrics regularly. In addition to the amount raised to date towards the total goal, here are a few stats that will help you evaluate how well the year is going.

Most donor/constituent management (DRM/CRM) systems will provide these numbers for you automatically.

- Total number of active donors (people who have given in the last 12 months)
- Total number of new donors to date in the fiscal year
- Average total gift amount
- Number of monthly donors

FUNDRAISING METRICS, Figure 10.

Donor Metrics as of (DATE)

Average Gift	Active Donors	New Donors	Monthly Donors
$100	315	23	30

At the end of the fiscal year, it is also important to evaluate donor attrition – how many people gave in the previous fiscal year, but not the current one. It is a major fundraising goal to build relationships and connections with people in ways that will inspire them to *continually* support your organization's mission.

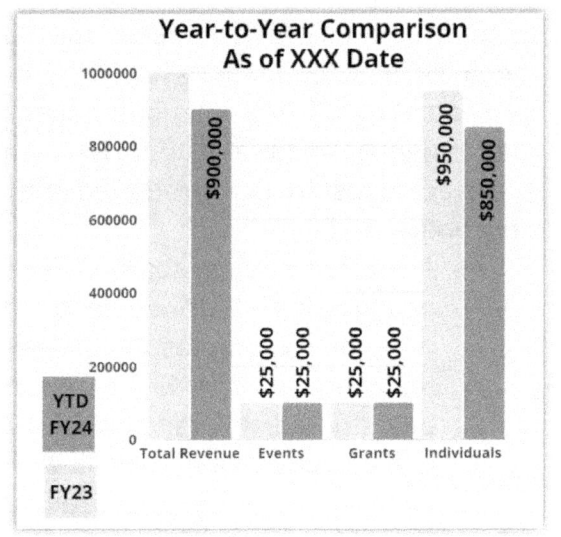

COMPARISON METRICS, Figure 11.

Year-to-year comparison by date and type of giving shown in Figure 11. is another way to determine how well your fundraising is going in the current fiscal year. Additionally, each month you should evaluate what percent of the total goal you've raised to date and then make adjustments as necessary, keeping the end goal in mind.

You will notice that funds are not raised in equal amounts split over each month of the year. Incoming funds tend to fluctuate throughout the year depending upon deadlines and what fundraising actions are scheduled for that time of year.

BUILDING THE INFRASTRUCTURE FOR SUCCESSFUL NONPROFIT FUNDRAISING

If you host any special events for the purpose of raising funds, you should keep track of running stats available leading up to the event. This will enable you to make any necessary adjustments in planning and execution of the event.

APPEAL* METRICS, Figure 13.

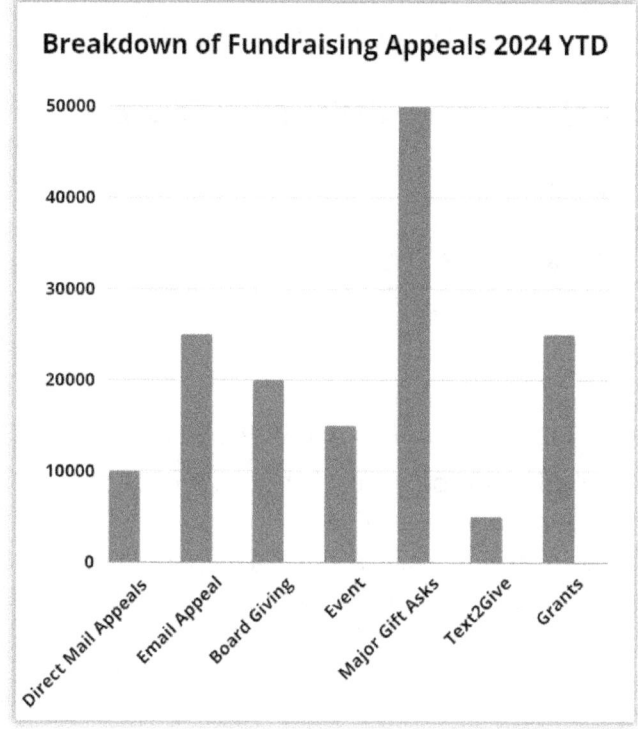

> **Upcoming Event Name**
>
> Tickets Sold: #
> Ticket Revenue: $
> Sponsors Sold: #
> Sponsor Revenue: $
> Additional Donations: $
>
> As of date:

EVENT METRICS, Figure 12.

We covered Development Plans in Chapter 6. The graph in Figure 13. is a visual representation of each category or type of fundraising. Keeping regular tabs on this information will keep you on target to reaching your goal.

In the Development Plan, you budgeted a total fundraising goal and broke it down into the giving channels through which you expect the gifts to be given. Tracking your appeal metrics will show you which types of appeal are on track, which are overperforming, and which are underperforming. *Keep in mind that the target is to reach the overall goal.* It matters more that you reach the total goal than that the gifts came in the predicted categories of giving.

*Various organizations categorize "campaigns" and "appeals" differently. The main thing is that you evaluate the vehicles you are using to ask for funds.

More Measurements of Effectiveness

Return on Investment (ROI) allows you to compare your own activities to each other. If one of your fundraising actions has a 20% ROI and another has a 40% ROI, then *all else being equal*, the activity with the 40% ROI is better. That is something you should take into account when determining which activities you want to repeat in future years. To calculate ROI, subtract expenses from total revenue to get net revenue, divide net revenue by expenses, then multiply by 100.[iii]

RETURN ON INVESTMENT, Figure 14.

$$\text{GROSS REVENUE} - \text{EXPENSES} = \text{NET REVENUE}$$

$$\text{THEN}$$

$$\text{NET REVENUE} / \text{EXPENSES} \times 100 = \text{ROI}$$

divide by   multiply by

COST PER DOLLAR RAISED, Figure 15.

Cost Per Dollar Raised (CPDR) enables you to compare your organization's actions with industry standards. If your direct mail campaign to active donors costs $0.50 for every dollar it raises, and the current industry standard for direct mail to current donors costs $0.25 for every dollar raised, you may want to consider whether the design or volume of your direct mail campaigns should be adjusted downward. To calculate CPDR, divide costs by gross revenue.[iv]

$$\text{COSTS} / \text{GROSS REVENUE} = \text{CPDR}$$

divide by

CHAPTER 8
Building Block - Development Committee

It is standard for nonprofit organization bylaws to list several board committees as a requirement of operation. The required committees are often Governance and Finance and sometimes include an Executive committee.

In addition to committees made necessary through bylaws, the majority of nonprofits also run a combination of additional committees, ad hoc committees, and/or short-term task forces. One such addition can be a Development/Fundraising committee.

> **Development Committee**
>
> The Development Committee partners with the development staff to plan and execute fundraising action for the organization. The committee is comprised of board members and non-board members; it reports to the board of directors. The committee works to assure that all fundraising actions are in line with the organization's strategic plan, adhere to state and federal law, and that the organization is upholding the Code of Ethics and Donor Bill of Rights.

Why a Development Committee?
Fundraising is more than a one-person job. Whether you have paid staff dedicated to fundraising or there is a board volunteer leading the efforts, they will need a lot of help. Raising funds to support mission delivery at the highest level is the responsibility of everyone at a nonprofit, especially the board of directors since part of their governance responsibility is to ensure their organizations are fiscally strong. One way to create a reliable support system for fundraising is to create a Development committee.

What is a Development Committee?
A Development committee is a group of people, who may or may not serve on the board of directors, who agree to champion fundraising for the organization and help motivate the board of directors in all things development related. These groups tend to meet monthly or bimonthly. There is no strict rule as to how this committee operates, but it should certainly identify goals that it wants to accomplish each time they gather so it doesn't become "just another meeting".

Generally, the staff member dedicated to fundraising is the person who organizes this committee. As the person who engages in fundraising as a profession, they are the best positioned to lay out strategy. Because they are also the main person/people responsible for doing the day-to-day work, they'll remind the committee to evaluate whether the agency has enough human resources to conduct any given project.

A Development committee is NOT dedicated to planning and hosting special events. In Chapter 6 we covered the creation of a Development Plan that outlines strategy and helps guide fundraising efforts throughout the year. *That* strategic work is what the committee will be supporting. Smaller task forces or groups may form to plan a special event, but will then dissolve once the event is over.

If your organization operates in a horizontal cooperative model, you may think that a Development committee goes against your ethos. In reality, such a committee can simply be considered a form of division of labor. It can be difficult to get groups of 13 to 15 (the full board) organized regularly, so you may have a group of five that meets more often to handle the groundwork.

Note: some organizations are loathe to call groups "committees", as they believe it smacks of institutional traditionalism and red tape. So, call the group whatever you'd like… a club, a task force, a flock of fundraisers. It doesn't matter what the group is called as long as they are willing to be the main champions of fundraising, both within and outside the organization, in support of the nonprofit's mission.

Scan this code to access a free sample Development Committee Job Description.

CHAPTER 9
Building Block - Policies, Procedures, & Ethics

The act of raising funds to support nonprofit organizations' missions not only involves best practices and industry standards, but it is also significantly regulated. Organizations must be aware of the practices, standards, and regulations that are involved in creating and maintaining a successful and transparent fundraising program that earns the trust and confidence of supporters and the community.

An important example of such regulation is that, currently in the U.S., 42 states plus the District of Columbia require nonprofits to register to be allowed to solicit funds in that state[v]. Additionally, some states have strict rules regarding fundraising activities such as raffles and auctions; other states have none. *It is up to each nonprofit organization to identify what laws and regulations govern their fundraising efforts.*

Many countries outside the U.S. also require that NPOs/NGOs follow significant regulations and guidelines. England and Wales, for example, have lengthy regulations outlined in the Charities Act 2011[vi]. It can be overwhelming, and often the smartest thing a nonprofit in any country can do is *seek legal and financial counsel from firms that specialize in nonprofit law and accounting*. Seeking counsel early on can save your organization from inadvertently operating out of compliance which, in the worst cases, can result in large fines and/or having the nonprofit's tax-exempt status revoked.

Who Needs to Know?
It is the responsibility of both the staff and the board of directors to be aware of the regulations, policies, and procedures that should be in place in order for the development program to operate efficiently, effectively, legally, equitably, and transparently. For organizations that have paid staff, the board can, for the most part, rely upon the executive director/chief executive officer and/or dedicated fundraising staff to keep current on and in compliance with fundraising-related regulations (though board members should still have enough knowledge to maintain appropriate oversight). For agencies that are volunteer run, the board of directors may choose to appoint several trustees to be accountable for this work.

An important item to note is that for a policy or standard operating procedure to exist, it must be documented. It is not enough for founders, board members, or staff to "just know" that the organization has intentions to follow a specific rule. It has to be in writing, and in many cases should also be formally approved by the board of directors.

Organizational Policies for Fundraising Use
There are organization-wide policies that are also a daily part of the fundraising process. Document retention is one example. Some documents should be saved/stored for seven years, some should be saved indefinitely. For example, according to the National Council on Nonprofits, donation checks should be kept forever[vii].

Another example of organizational policies that should be followed, and potentially even enhanced for use in fundraising, are those covering privacy and data security. As of 2024, privacy laws in many U.S. states are becoming stricter. The Nonprofit Alliance (tnpa.org) is a good resource for keeping up with legislative changes and requirements. TPNA is also a source to consult for any upcoming regulations pertaining to the use of artificial intelligence (AI) in fundraising and donor communications/interactions.

In addition to *organization-wide* policies such as those related to human resources, financial investments, dedication to diversity, equity, inclusion, access, and justice; social media use, data security, press relations, disaster preparedness, and compliance with the Sarbanes-Oxley Act of 2002 (document retention and destruction, whistleblower protections[viii]), it is also important to document policies *specifically for fund development*.

Fundraising-Specific Policy
One of the most important policies nonprofits can have is a Gift Acceptance Policy. A Gift Acceptance Policy defines the types of gifts the organization can/will accept, what they won't accept, and what would need board approval to accept. For example, a nonprofit might accept gifts of cash, in-kind donations (non-cash) of items that help them operate, and gifts of appreciated stock. But they may decline to take certain types of gifts in kind, such as artwork. They may elect to accept gifts of real estate only under certain, very strict conditions.

Gift Acceptance Policies in most cases should include an ethics/morals/values clause. Such a clause states that the organization may decline any gift that is not in line with its mission or values. An example of a gift that might be contrary to an organization's mission would be if an organization that serves people with developmental disabilities declines to take donations from chemical companies that manufacture specific chemicals that are scientifically considered to *cause* developmental disabilities. That may sound like an obvious choice. But what about organizations that serve people who are in addiction recovery? Should they accept donations from liquor distillers or distributors? It is up to each individual organization, but it is good to decide ahead of time what your policy will be so that you don't have to scramble when such a situation arises. Having a Gift Acceptance Policy can save your fundraising team/volunteers and board trustees a lot of headaches.

Sample Gift Acceptance Policies can be found in a number of places online. One such source is the National Council of Nonprofits (councilofnonprofits.org). Regardless of how you draft your organization's policies, it is a good practice to have them vetted by legal counsel before use.

Procedures
Like policies, it is also a good practice to document procedures and processes from the beginning. They may change over time and need updating, but it is tremendously helpful to staff and volunteers to know if there are certain procedures or processes they should follow.

The need for procedures (sometimes called Standard Operating Procedures or SOPs) crops up just about every place within an organization. Examples from the development department include, but are not limited to:

- **Gift processing for offline donations** – Who opens the mail, what happens to the checks, how are they entered into the donor/customer/constituent relationship management system (DRM/CRM), how do they flow to accounting, etc.?
- **Gift receipting** – Once gifts are in the DRM/CRM, who sends thank you and acknowledgement letters and in what timeframe, as well as what tax language should be included for which types of gifts?
- **New donor welcome and/or monthly giving levels** – Some organizations choose to automatically send specific communications to new donors and to have certain deliverables at various levels of monthly giving (such as a welcome letter, newsletter, card from a board member, or tchotchke). It is good to have the levels, timing, and actions documented for all to follow.

- **Data Entry into DRM/CRM** – A database is as only as good as the information entered. It is important to determine how you want the data to be recorded – what information goes into what fields and in what format (often called data mapping). Define what will be referred to as a Campaign, an Appeal, and/or a Fund (how you assign these may be dictated by what brand DRM/CRM you use, as each software product has their own spin on such tracking). *How* you decide to do it doesn't matter as much as *being consistent* in the way you do it. Documenting your desired method of entering data will help make sure your data is clean, which enables you to find, compare, and report donations with accuracy, which in turn helps you build relationships with your constituents at a deeper level.

> JUST BECAUSE SOMETHING IS TECHNICALLY LEGAL DOESN'T MAKE IT ETHICAL. KEEP AN EYE OUT FOR SUCH SITUATIONS AT YOUR NONPROFIT.

Ethics

There are degrees, classes, debates, books, and forums that dissect all manner of ethical questions in minute detail. For the purpose of this book, I'm going to boil it down to three main concepts.

1. *Ethical actions for nonprofits are not the same as ethical actions at for-profit companies.* As most boards of directors are made up of unpaid volunteers who are businesspeople from the community, this is an important distinction to make. For example, in a for-profit business, it is generally considered ethical to pay an employee on a commission basis; in nonprofit sector fundraising, it is not. In the for-profit sector, many businesses expect some type of reciprocity when they do business with a person or company; in the non-profit sector, this type of quid pro quo arrangement is considered unethical.
2. *What is considered ethical and acceptable may change depending on where you are operating.* In South Africa and Kenya, for example, NGOs are often funded via foundation grants more than by individual donors. In many cases the NGOs have membership bodies that vote on major organizational initiatives at an annual meeting and boards of directors are less involved in governance. There, it is an accepted practice for nonprofits to recruit board members and then to pay all of the expenses for those board members to attend conferences in other countries and on different continents. Historically in the United States and Canada, an arrangement like this *could* be construed as the trustee benefitting from their position as a board member by receiving free international travel; such personal benefit goes against one of the most basic tenets of board service. There is, however, currently some discussion in the U.S. regarding the

potential value of offering compensation (which could create liability issues) or of reimbursing for board member travel expenses and other expenses that may be prohibitive to some potential trustees.[ix]

Some U.S. organizations decide to pay certain types of board member expenses because it is a way to make their boards more equitable. If trustees are not required to incur large amounts of expenses to serve on the board, it can decrease the possibility that the NGOs are "pricing out" good board members because of inability to pay. The National Council of Nonprofits is a good resource for information on this complex topic.[x] I am not suggesting that either setup is right or wrong, just that they are different based on the country and culture.

3. *What is considered ethical is evolving as the independent sector evolves.* For example, many nonprofit organizations are working towards there being an equitable relationship between funders, the nonprofit and its staff, board trustees, and the clients that are served. They wish to diminish the type of power imbalance that has long existed where wealthy donors were exalted above all else, and where their donations *may* have given them undue influence over the organization's actions.

These nonprofits are likely to use a stronger magnifying glass when examining all elements of interactions between the participant groups. This is another example of a place where it is good to document the organization's values and any particular ethical positions the NGO takes, so that it is easier for staff and volunteers to make decisions in line with the organization's core values.

There are two long-standing documents that have defined ethics in fundraising in the U.S., Canada, and in many countries globally. Both can be used as tools by nonprofits and their staff as a starting place. They are the **Code of Ethical Standards** and the **Donor Bill of Rights**, both of which can be accessed through the Association of Fundraising Professionals (AFP) at www.afpglobal.org. More information about evolving practices will be covered in Chapter 10.

EXAMPLE OF HOW THE THREE WORK TOGETHER

POLICY = TO BACKGROUND CHECK ANYONE OVER THE AGE OF 18 WHO WILL COME IN CONTACT WITH CHILDREN.

PROCEDURE = HOW AND WHEN SPECIFIC THINGS WILL HAPPEN. FOR EXAMPLE:
- BEFORE A STAFF OR VOLUNTEER POSITION OFFER IS EXTENDED, THE APPLICANT WILL FOLLOW BACKGROUND CHECK STEPS OUTLINED BY THE ORGANIZATION.
- ONCE THE CHECK IS RETURNED, THE ORGANIZATION WILL EVALUATE IT AGAINST THEIR DEFINED CRITERIA.
- IF PASSED, THE POSITION WILL BE OFFERED AND THE RESULTS OF THE BACKGROUND CHECK WILL BE STORED IN A SPECIFIC LOCATION FOR A DEFINED AMOUNT OF TIME.
- FEDERAL AND STATE BACKGROUND CHECKS WILL BE REPEATED ANNUALLY.

ETHICS = IT IS POSSIBLE THAT THE STATE ONLY REQUIRES BACKGROUND CHECKS TO BE CONDUCTED AT THE TIME OF HIRE OR WHEN A VOLUNTEER STARTS WITH THE ORGANIZATION. THE STATE MAY ALSO NOT REQUIRE BOARD MEMBERS TO SUBMIT TO BACKGROUND CHECKS BECAUSE THEY ARE SELDOM IN CONTACT WITH THE CHILDREN. BUT THE ORGANIZATION DETERMINES IT IS THEIR POLICY TO BACKGROUND CHECK BOARD MEMBERS AND TO REPEAT ALL CHECKS ANNUALLY IN AN EFFORT TO FULFILL THEIR DUTY OF CARE TO KEEP THE CHILDREN THEY WORK WITH AS SAFE AS POSSIBLE.

ONE BOARD MEMBER, WHO IS ALSO A MAJOR DONOR, DOES NOT WANT TO SUBMIT TO A BACKGROUND CHECK BECAUSE IT IS NOT LEGALLY REQUIRED BY THE STATE. THE NONPROFIT MAINTAINS ITS POSITION THAT ALL BOARD MEMBERS WILL BE BACKGROUND CHECKED ANNUALLY IN ORDER TO BE ELIGIBLE TO KEEP THEIR POSITION - WITHOUT EXCEPTION.

RESULT = HAPPY, SAFE KIDS AND AN EXCELLENT EFFORT TOWARDS RISK MITIGATION.

CHAPTER 10
Building Block - Fundraising Evolution

The ways people give to support nonprofit missions are changing. So too are the philosophies organizations have about how they interact with people and communities in their efforts to gain support for and to deliver on their missions. It is important that nonprofit organizations keep current with and evaluate new schools of thought as they arise, so they can always be in tune with the needs and desires of their stakeholders (not to chase trends, mind you, but to be able to make well-informed decisions).

A *philosophy* might not seem like a tangible item that you'd normally picture when thinking of infrastructure, but it *is* foundational to how your staff, board, and volunteers operate - especially in the context of creating a positive decision-making structure and a Culture of Philanthropy surrounding your fundraising efforts.

Historical Focus of Fundraising & Leadership

Many established nonprofits, especially those that are headquartered in the U.S. and Canada, have for decades tried to focus almost exclusively on high-net-worth individuals and granting foundations as their main sources of philanthropic income. That doesn't mean that all of their supporters gave at mega-gift levels, just that major givers and foundations were seen as a bit of a holy grail and were therefore treated with a liberal dose of reverence. Large gifts and grants are and will remain an important part of funding mission delivery and capital projects (buildings and other high-dollar items). They also play important roles when providing seed funding for pilot programs and forward-thinking initiatives in the nonprofit sector.

However, in the effort to surround their nonprofit agencies with such holy-grail donors (both through giving and invitations to board leadership positions), organizations have, in some cases, created situations where those potential donors have an inordinate amount of influence over the nonprofit's actions. It is that level of attention and influence that should be reviewed carefully.

Today, more and more nonprofits are making the effort to treat those who give large gifts or grants more as investors and partners instead of magnanimous saviors to those less fortunate. The industry as a whole is working on doing a better job of valuing donors/supporters at all levels of giving, of treating all with respect and appreciation instead of honoring just a few with reverence.

Equity & Inclusion

Additionally, donors/supporters and the nonprofits themselves are gaining a heightened awareness of the role diversity, equity, inclusion, access, and justice play in nonprofit work and philanthropy and are seeing somewhat of a dearth of those elements in the sector as it exists today.

Some potential donors now look at nonprofits for evidence of diversity of all types (e.g., gender, age, race, education level, LGBTQ+ identification, geography, lived experience, and many other characteristics by which people may self-identify) on both their boards of directors and within their staff at all levels - *including leadership positions*. Some potential donors may even inquire about the nonprofit's investment policies for any reserve or endowment funds it may have, to see if the organization's investments match their stated values.

Smart organizational leaders and boards of directors who may historically have made decisions on behalf of people who were not represented "in the room" are now taking corrective action to help ensure their organizations are more inclusive and representative. These efforts have been slow to take hold at some organizations. So, if you represent a new nonprofit organization, you have a fantastic opportunity to ensure that your organization is truthfully infused with diversity, equity, inclusion, access, and justice from day one.

In addition to looking for evidence of diversity, inclusion, et al., some potential supporters also look for salary transparency and pay equity. Such scrutiny by supporters is teaching nonprofit organizations that it is necessary to reflect the communities in which they work and whom they serve, and that they should evaluate all of their own actions for fairness and equity.

The operations of the entire organization affect the nonprofit's ability to successfully raise philanthropic dollars. Sound, strategic, and transparent governance practices, strong staff and board leadership, quality and impact of programs, community reputation, sound future planning, and equitable treatment of stakeholders (including staff) all play a role.

Changing Fundraising Methodologies

In terms of *how* to drive your organization's development efforts, there are fundraising methodologies and schools of thought that lead in several different directions.

Previously, as described above, the most popular and long-prevailing methodology focused on donors and foundations. As authors Anne Bergeron and Eugene R. Tempel describe in Achieving Fundraising Excellence, "The field of fundraising has long taught that philanthropy is a donor-directed choice, motivated by the interests and intentions of the giver."[xi]

It was common to place donors, especially givers of large gifts, on a pedestal at the center of a nonprofit's universe and to work out from there. Over the last few years, a popular alternative methodology has arisen that removes the pedestal from under the donor and focuses on the power of communities as a whole to identify, deliver, and fund solutions.

As an example of this evolution, we can look to two documents. In Chapter 9 I shared the URL to access the longstanding **Donor Bill of Rights** created by the Association of Fundraising Professionals and its many partners that, as the name suggests, defines safeguards for nonprofits' donors. Alternatively (additionally), you can now find Bergeron & Tempel's **Proposed Beneficiary Bill of Rights** in the 5th Edition of Achieving Fundraising Excellence, Chapter 2. The Proposed Beneficiary Bill of Rights focuses on responsive philanthropy that is inclusive and listens to the needs of the community above all else.

Human Focused Fundraising®
The two schools of thought described above can be generalized as "donor focused" and "community focused". Personally, I like to consider the ideal scenario to be a human-focused approach. Human Focused Fundraising® (HFF) encompasses the people involved at every level of the process of fundraising to support needs that are identified by inclusive and representative groups. The role and impact of donors isn't devalued, it is just placed in a more level context with the other groups of stakeholders. In this model, donors don't *determine* what communities need; they *help address* what communities need.

Human Focused Fundraising®:
- **Engages appropriately representative and qualified humans to determine needs and posit, test, and implement solutions**.
    - It is true that the act of fundraising is undertaken to secure funds to enable mission delivery. It is also true that we want fundraising to secure dollars for the *right* mission-delivery components that most appropriately address real needs.

- o Fundraising is about listening, questioning, and working to connect people who want to help with needs that match their passion. If an organization's programs are selected/directed by a small, homogeneous group of people who do not have lived experience, practical experience, or relevant academic expertise, then it runs the risk of creating programs that are not best suited for what the community needs.
- **Requires diverse and representative governing leadership.**
    - o The board of directors is responsible for the strategic direction of the organization and should be heavily involved in fundraising. The trustees are also, in fact, donors themselves (at whatever level is significant to them personally).
    - o For a board to make appropriate strategic decisions on behalf of the organization, they must be truly representative of all the organization's wide array of stakeholders, as described in the Equity and Inclusion section above.
- **Employs broad, inclusive fundraising strategies that honor the triadic relationship between funders, nonprofit organizations, and the individuals and communities served.**
    - o In the same way that organizations have historically operated and governed from a relatively narrow perspective, some have also clung to a seemingly immovable set of principles that drive the way they seek funding to support their missions.

        It's time to normalize the fact that different generations and varied demographics of people like to engage with nonprofits in disparate ways. Some like to have a close partnership with organizations they support, some like philanthropy to be a part of their social life, others prefer to remain at arm's length while supporting through purchases of cause-marketed goods. Still others enjoy tying philanthropy to pop culture and influencers they follow. None of these are wrong. They simply represent a variety of people's styles.
    - o In addition to the methods nonprofits use to *raise* funds, they should also consider the vehicles they offer to *receive* funds. Gone are the days where you can expect donors to simply either write a check or give via the organization's website.

        As nonprofits evolve to be more inclusive of all types and ages of donors, they must also adjust to the ways those supporters want to give (not the way they respond to fundraising efforts, but literally the physical method by which they pay). Currently, organizations that accept donations by credit card, PayPal, Apple Pay, Venmo, Cash App, Zelle, social media platforms, electronic money transfers (ACH), stock transfer, and possibly even cryptocurrency are showing that they are listening to how people want to give and are making themselves available on those platforms. (As technology changes, these methods of receiving donations will also change, so it is important to keep up on the latest tools.)

o Regardless of the ways nonprofits ask for and receive funds, what makes them truly trustworthy in many supporters' eyes are their efforts to value all stakeholders equally. Yes, they may have different types of relationships with financial supporters than they do with clients, but the truly inclusive organization's actions show that they don't create an invisible hierarchy that dictates that they value one group over another.

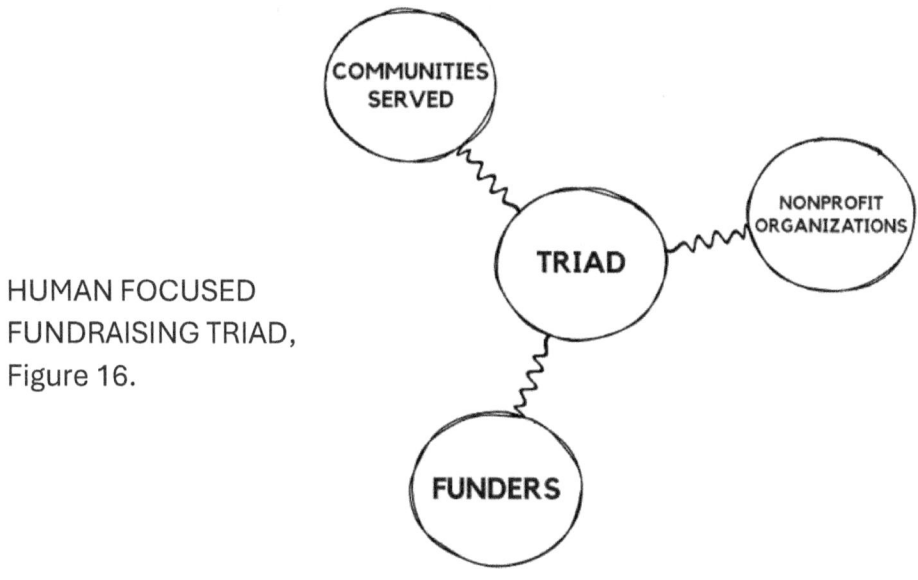

HUMAN FOCUSED FUNDRAISING TRIAD, Figure 16.

HUMAN FOCUSED FUNDRAISING®

Now is the time to leave some of the rigidity of the traditional fundraising process behind. *That is not to say you shouldn't be strategic, organized, and professional, but that nonprofits must be willing to incorporate flexibility into their core tenets.*

Let us create an industry-wide ecosystem that encompasses the issues and problems to be addressed, viable solutions, and how to secure the funding needed to deliver those solutions.

The most important aspect of this more evolved sector is the recognition that humans are involved at every stage and are all stakeholders equally crucial to the process. Without equitable human interaction, the industry that provides society's safety net can end up being as much a part of the problem as it is the solution.

 Your approach to fundraising can be from an HFF, donor-focused, or community-focused perspective; what matters most is that your style of fundraising and organizational leadership matches the representative values your organization holds at its core. As long as nonprofits are intentional about including the right people at every level, showing gratitude for the part everyone plays, and treating everyone involved with an attitude of equity, they're laying the groundwork for an incredible future in the nonprofit sector.

SUMMARY

The nonprofit sector is made up of people and organizations who accomplish great things. They create art and music, safeguard the environment, work for justice in the systems that govern society, and provide safety-net services for those in emergency need. Hopefully moving forward, nonprofits will also be an increasingly valuable part of proactively addressing core issues *before* they become emergency needs.

The prevailing governance and funding structures that are unique to nonprofit organizations, and that have been in place for many decades, have inadvertently created *some* scenarios where fundraising to support nonprofit missions isn't always conducted as strategically and equitably as it should be for work that is so important to our society.

Fundraising should be a big part of planning and operations from the beginning of an organization's existence; it shouldn't be treated as a necessary evil.

Whether you're building a new nonprofit or reorganizing an existing fundraising department, the **10 Essential Building Blocks for Nonprofit Fundraising** will help you build the strategic infrastructure needed to ensure you have a successful, professional fundraising program that is built to last – and to scale with your organization as it grows. The better the tools your organization makes available to staff and volunteers, the best chance you have for fundraising success early and often!

10 Essential Building Blocks for Nonprofit Fundraising

- Case for Support
- Culture of Philanthropy
- Staffing
- Goals & Budgeting
- Technology
- Development Methods & Plans
- Performance Indicators
- Development Committee
- Policies, Procedures, & Ethics
- Fundraising Evolution

GLOSSARY

Case for Support – *(n.)* A document that articulates the reason the organization exists, what situation or problem in the community that it addresses, and why it needs and is deserving of financial support. It is often used as a supporting tool to share information with potential larger donors. It highlights details that both inform on financials and illustrate the mission.

Case Statement – *(n.)* A phrase sometimes used interchangeably with "Case for Support", but is commonly accepted to be a short summary, sometimes as little as two or three sentences, of the Case for Support.

Cause Marketing – *(n.)* A situation where for-profit brands/companies partner with nonprofit organizations for mutual benefit. The nonprofit benefits from wider exposure and from funds donated as an element of the partnership. The for-profit company benefits from perception of goodwill and community investment. There is likely also a tax-deduction benefit to the company.

Constituent Relationship Management System (CRM) – *(n.)* A database that holds contact details on donors and prospects. The system allows nonprofits to track all interactions with people in their CRM. More sophisticated CRMs integrate with online fundraising pages that accept donations. *See also, Customer Relationship Management System (CRM) and Donor Relationship Management System (DRM).*

Cost Per Dollar Raised (CPDR) – *(n.)* A performance measurement that calculates how much money it costs an organization to raise each philanthropic dollar received.

Culture of Philanthropy – *(n.)* A state in which an organization embraces fundraising as a positive part of the organization and integrates fundraising into all areas, including the board of directors, paid staff, and volunteers.

Customer Relationship Management System (CRM) – *(n.)* A database that holds contact details on donors and prospects. The system allows nonprofits to track all interactions with people in their CRM. More sophisticated CRMs integrate with online fundraising pages that accept donations. *See also, Constituent Relationship Management System (CRM) and Donor Relationship Management System (DRM).*

Development – *(n.)* The description used to encompass all of the actions of fundraising for philanthropic dollars (i.e., engaging in fund development).
(adj.) The general term used to describe the department of people who raise philanthropic dollars in support of a nonprofit's mission (i.e., development department).

Donor Relationship Management System (DRM) – *(n.)* A database that holds contact details on donors and prospects. The system allows nonprofits to track all interactions with people in their DRM. More sophisticated DRMs integrate with online fundraising pages that accept donations. *See also, Constituent Relationship Management System (CRM) and Customer Relationship Management System (CRM).*

Equity – *(n.)* Equity refers to fairness and justice and is distinguished from equality: Whereas equality means providing the same to all, equity means recognizing that we do not all start from the same place and must acknowledge and make adjustments to imbalances.[xii]

Fundraising – *(n.)* The act of securing financial support for a nonprofit organization through philanthropic means.

Goal – *(n.)*
    Organizational – The overall dollar amount of income an organization targets for a fiscal year. It generally includes all funding sources.

    Fundraising Departmental – The dollar amount of income that is targeted/expected to be raised by philanthropic means.

Human Focused Fundraising® – *(n.)* A fundraising model created by Phil-Com that promotes an equitable, triadic partnership between funders, nonprofit organizations, and the clients served.

Metrics – *(n.)* Numerical data collected for the purpose of evaluation.

Quid Pro Quo – *(n.)* The literal Latin translation is "something for something". It is a situation where one party expects something in return for what they've given or done.

Return on Investment (ROI) – *(n.)* Compares how much you earned on something to how much you invested in it.

Sarbanes-Oxley – *(n.)* The Sarbanes-Oxley Act was signed into law on July 30, 2002. It was passed in response to the corporate and accounting scandals of Enron, Tyco, and others of 2001 and 2002; the law's purpose is to rebuild public trust in America's corporate sector.[xiii]

Social Enterprise – *(n.)* The situation when a business seeks to maximize its profits while at the same time maximizing benefits to society.[xiv] Often use the sale of goods or services to fund social programs.

Visit: phil-com.com

Follow Tracy at: linkedin.com/in/tracyvanderneck

Read Tracy's articles on: nonprofitpro.com/author/tracyvanderneck

Scan for **BOOK CLUB QUESTIONS**:

REFERENCES

[i] Joyaux, S.,(retrieval date, 3/2024) "Building a Culture of Philanthropy in Your Organization", Joyaux Associates

[ii] Budget Template (retrieval date 7/2024). https://www.nhnonprofits.org/resources/budget-template
https://www.nhnonprofits.org/resources/budget-template

[iii] Stiver, S., (retrieval date, 3/2024), "How to Calculate Fundraising ROI", Causevox

[iv] Warner, G., (2020), "Cost Per Dollar Raised, What it Means and How to Stay on Top of It", Fundraising Report Card, by Marketsmart

[v] Affinity Fundraising Registration Map (retrieval date 5/2024), https://www.fundraisingregistration.com/resources/states-requiring-registration-map.php

[vi] Council on Foundations, (retrieval date 5/2024), "Nonprofit Law in England and Wales".

[vii] National Council on Nonprofits (retrieval date 5/2024), "Document Retention Policies for Nonprofits". https://www.councilofnonprofits.org/running-nonprofit/governance-leadership/document-retention-policies-nonprofits

[viii] Cohen, R., (2012) "Sarbanes-Oxley: 10 Years Later", Nonprofit Quarterly.

[ix] Neo Law Group, (retrieval date 8/2024), "Compensating Nonprofit Board Members",

[x] National Council of Nonprofits, (retrieval date 8/2024), "Can Board Members Be Paid?", https://www.councilofnonprofits.org/running-nonprofit/governance-leadership/can-board-members-be-paid

[xi] Bergeron, Temple, (2022), "Philanthropic Concepts for Fundraising", Achieving Excellence in Fundraising, 5th Edition. John Wiley & Sons, Inc.

[xii] National Association of Colleges & Employers, (retrieval date 7/2024), https://www.naceweb.org/about-us/equity-definition

[xiii] BoardSource, (2006), "The Sarbanes-Oxley Act and Implications for Nonprofit Organizations"

[xiv] Investopedia, (2022), (Retrieval date 8/2024), https://www.investopedia.com/terms/s/social-enterprise.asp

www.ingramcontent.com/pod-product-compliance
Lightning Source LLC
Chambersburg PA
CBHW060327240426
43665CB00047B/2809